Y0-EGZ-976

WITHDRAWN FROM
CANISIUS COLLEGE LIBRARY

THE LONE
ADVENTURER

Among the Other Books in the Same Field
by Stanton A. Coblentz

VERSE

Selected Short Poems
Garnered Sheaves
The Pageant of Man
The Pageant of the New World
Time's Travelers
Winds of Chaos
From a Western Hilltop
Songs of the Redwoods
Redwood Poems
Green Vistas
Out of Many Songs
Atlantis and Other Poems
Songs by the Wayside
The Merry Hunt and Other Poems
Shadows on a Wall
The Mountain of the Sleeping Maiden
Senator Goose and Other Rhymes
Aesop's Fables (rhymed versions)

PROSE

The Poetry Circus
An Editor Looks at Poetry
My Life in Poetry

The
Lone Adventurer

New Edition, Extensively Revised

by

Stanton A. Coblentz

1975

THE REDWOOD PRESS

San Jose   California

Copyright 1927 The Unicorn Press
Copyright 1954 Stanton A. Coblentz
Copyright © 1975 on foreword and revisions
by Stanton A. Coblentz

Library of Congress Catalog Card No. 75-11029

All rights reserved by
THE REDWOOD PRESS
5380 Cribari Crest
San Jose, California 95135

PS
3505
.O144
L6
1975

Printed by
Harlo Press, 16721 Hamilton Avenue, Detroit, Michigan 48203

CANISIUS COLLEGE LIBRARY
BUFFALO N Y.

TO EMILY

*The Light of
my latter years
this book
is affectionately dedicated*

FOREWORD TO THE REVISED EDITION

As I look over this largely rewritten and somewhat shortened version of a poem first published in 1927, I realize that I risk being branded a literary heretic if not an anachronism. In these days of prose and practicality, few things are further from the average mind than the long poem, and particularly the romantic long poem. And yet my departure from current trends calls for no apology. In most lands in which the written word has had vogue, and in all ages before our own since the invention of language, the long poem and not least the imaginative long poem has been a dominant and frequently *the* dominant form of literature. One thinks offhand of the great of the ages, from Homer and Virgil through Dante and Camoens and Goethe and England's Chaucer, Spenser, Shakespeare, and Milton; and one recognizes that their choice of a vehicle was dictated not only by the modes and conventions of the times but by an underlying fitness—the fact that in no other medium than narrative or dramatic poetry could the authors have expressed their thoughts fully and impressively and with the grandeur of great utterance.

For poetry, however degraded it may currently have become, has within it the possibility of a compression and a finality of utterance, an illumination and a flow and beauty and at times a magnificence surpassing even that of the most inspired prose. Hence it may provide a deep and memorable experience and exert an influence possible in no other medium. It is for this reason that persons versed in the older poetry have been able to memorize long passages from Shakespeare, Keats, Tennyson, and many another, and have kept them locked within their hearts as treasures upon which to draw time after time. It is for this reason, also, that Shelley was able to call poets the "unacknowledged legislators of the world."

In presenting the revised edition of *The Lone Adventurer,* needless to say, I make no pretense to follow in the footsteps of any of the poets named above. All that I do claim is that long poems, based on narrative themes, deserve much more of an audience than they have been receiving, and may fill a place that no other form of writing can occupy. But they cannot have an audience unless some of us, within the limits of our abilities, continue to write and to publish in this medium. It is unnecessary, in my view, that the poet, in his preoccupation with modern themes, delve into such things as Freudian or Jungian psychology, or fill his lines with high-rise apartments and super-highways, jet planes and factory towers, and all the other paraphernalia of modern life— such transient matters may be better handled in prose. But an imagined hero, moving in lands that may or may not be imaginary, may have elements of the everlasting, and may cast revealing rays upon our own era and ways of life and thought. And in an allegorical story, reflections may shine from the realities that lie beyond all the shifts of time and form and space.

Such, at least, have been the views guiding me in the revised version of *The Lone Adventurer,* as in its original writing. I realize, of course, that a poet can never fully fulfill his aspirations, and I make no claim except of writing in a mode which deserves more attention than it has been receiving, and which, properly treated, may give both inspiration and pleasure and shed light upon avenues that seem new but are actually as old as the sunbeams twinkling on a dewy morning and the dazzle of starlight in a moonless sky.

—S.A.C.

January, 1975

CONTENTS

Foreword to the Revised Edition

THE LONE
ADVENTURER

To follow knowledge like a sinking star
Beyond the utmost bound of human thought.

— *Tennyson, "Ulysses"*

Part I

IN THE COURT OF THE KING

I

Beyond what sea no Homer's chant has told,
And past what mountains we can only guess,
A world-commanding empire once unrolled,
Bounded by blanks of mapless wilderness.
August as Rome, in power scarcely less,
She trained her conquering valiants, horde on horde,
When still no Latin warrior raised the sword.

With darts of iron and catapults of fire
Helmud, her grandest sovereign, smote his foes.
In smoke of villages and fields his ire
Spouted to heaven, while his bolts and bows
Levelled high cities and he took a pose
Of clanking splendor, and was deified
For rearing altars to his kingdom's pride.

But not alone he led in might of steel —
He knew the sunlike force of gentle ways,
And stamped, in smiling patronage, his seal
On busts and monuments and scrolls and plays,
So that the land might chorus forth his praise:
"He nurtured flowers of knowledge and of art,
And fashioned music for the wounded heart."

Castles with windows bright as eyes of flame,
And crystal galleries, domes of purple glass,
And irised courts and temples bore his name,
While cavaliers and maids, begemmed, would pass —
Butterfly children of the royal class,
Who danced and feasted, and would lounge night-long
In marble aisles of revelry and song.

"Lord of All Lands" they called King Helmud, yet
His bowl of joy ran never to the brim.
More lingering than pleasure, one regret
Often in secret made his eyes grow dim,
And when the midnight silence closed on him
Sometimes his gaze would seek the stars, in vain
Courting mute solace for unspoken pain.

He grieved for one, the eldest of his line,
The prince Lodalga, who in later years
Would burn sweet incense in the family shrine
And rule when Helmud left to join his peers.
But this strange lad, defying threats and tears,
Seemed not to hear the imperial summons call,
And scarcely cared to be a king at all.

A sad, shy youth, he loved the wooded ways,
And loved to rove the palace park alone,
To watch red sunsets smoldering out in haze
Or walk where ragged moonlit fountains shone.
But he could see no glory in a throne,
And held a bird or bluebell might create
Marvels to shame the brazen seats of state.

"Oh, let me know the world, the fields, the stars,
Still lakes and leafy solitudes!" he cried.
"Let perfumed lords be drawn in silver cars,
A gloss without, and hollowness inside.
But I would wander where the high winds ride
On houseless prairies, far from all the mass
Hedged in this wilderness of paint and glass."

Helmud, disheartened at such wilful speech,
Would smile a twisted smile, and ruefully say,
"My son, the gods have put within your reach
Honors for which the envious millions pray.
And would you fling them pebble-like away?
A world salaams before you — why ignore
The glittering showers lords and priests outpour?"

Innumerable the weavings Helmud used
To school Lodalga in the princely arts.
"Come, practice how to hurl the battle darts
And wield the sabre!" But the youth refused,
Pleading, "The cult of arms is much abused,
And there are myriad crafts I'd sooner know
Than how to drive a rapier through a foe."

Then Helmud, in dismay but patient still,
Directed, "Let us try a milder training.
We'll nourish your negotiating skill
In some far kingdom, where a rival's reigning.
And there, by suave pretense and polished feigning,
You'll put our minions on the throne, and be
Conqueror by adroit diplomacy."

But once again the fractious youth demurred.
"What matter if our empire wane or grow?
The eternal stars shall circle round unstirred,
And, when our palace ruins crumble low,
The wind shall rustle past, and never know.
And kingdoms dead, and kingdoms yet to come,
Shall drift as dust beneath time's careless thumb."

II

Sad-eyed, with brow that wrinkled, Helmud now
Sought his advisers in the council room,
And in slow, laden phrases told them how
Some imp forbade Lodalga to assume
The sword and crown. Then all sat stooped in gloom,
And long, with lips downturned, they mulled and schemed
How the unruly prince might be redeemed:

Till one, the sagest of the party, said,
"Let youth itself, O Sire, become your aid.
Dismiss your gray-haired councillors; instead,
Go seek some mischievous-eyed and comely maid.
With each coy tossing of her prankish head
She'll have more power to mold and rule the lad
Than all our laws and mandates ever had."

"Good!" cried the king. And with no more debate
He bade his emissaries scour the land
To find some peerless lady as the mate
Of Prince Lodalga . . . Soon, at his command,
Proud maidens, plumed to win the prince's hand,
Paraded through the throne-room, one by one,
While Helmud sought the fairest for his son.

Dazzling were they as visions of romance
Young lovers dream in secret. Not a few
Boasted the gift of royal blood — a chance
Which made them queenlier in the monarch's view.
And in the end the king selected two
Who by their arts and beauty might essay
To wean Lodalga from his witless way.

And that the pair might cast a sorceress light,
Charming the youth to be their lord and slave,
Helmud concealed them from the prince's sight
Till an appointed royal ball he gave,
When flags and strings of picture-lamps would wave,
So that, in gala mood, the wayward son
From the two maids might choose the Matchless One.

Baron and princess, priest and battle lord
Streamed to the palace on the festal day.
And, bright as autumn-painted leaves, they poured
Into the state-room, where the drums made gay.
Then on the silken sofa-rugs they lay,
While gold-plumed eunuchs, an obsequious line,
Stood waiting to bestow the meat and wine.

High in their midst, each on an emerald throne,
Waving a peacock fan with languid grace,
The honored ladies like twin pheasants shone,
Birdlike of posture, flower-fair of face.
"Oh, to be stationed in their happy place!"
Many a maid in blushing envy said.
"Oh, that the prince might smile on me instead!"

Meantime the king, before the feast began,
Surveyed the lanterned halls in high content,
Laughing with all, a blithe and gracious man,
Till for the youthful prince at last he sent.
And then cold winds snuffed out his merriment.
"Lodalga" — so the servant's message ran —
"Would like to come, but don't believe he can."

"He can — and must!" roared Helmud, with a frown
That made his slaves drop trembling out of sight.
"Is it Lodalga's head that holds the crown?
And dares he question if my ways be right?
Then like an arrow let my judgment smite!
Go, call the scapegrace! Say we'll speak alone
In the dark court-room just beyond the throne!"

Threatening like a lightning-laden cloud,
Helmud withdrew; and searching out his son
He spoke, in tones imperiously loud,
"Freedom, Lodalga, is no thing to shun!
So be not foolish — let my will be done!
But can it be you'd have the hardihood
To quench the lamp I've lighted for your good?"

"It is not hardihood," the prince denied.
"Father, I sorrow if I cause you pain.
Yet sooner would I bid you toss aside
Even my life, like dead leaves down a drain,
Than let you take the hope of love in vain
By choosing, with a cool, judicial glance,
To thread for me the rose-lanes of romance.

"Not that your chosen girls may not be fair
And merit some far worthier prize than I.
But could I hold them precious? Could I stare
With them, night-haunted, at the starlit sky?
Or should I not, still lonely, pine and sigh
To usher some unknown through violet bowers
When March winds flutter round the apple flowers?"

"Be not misled, my son," King Helmud urged.
"I too was young, and well recall a time
When lovelorn visions like high billows surged
Then sank to ripples, while the smoke and grime
Of teeming life filled all their luminous clime.
Bubbles will burst when stony facts commence —
Come, join our party like a lad of sense."

"I shall not join!" the stubborn prince replied.
"To meet the damsels face to face would be
To cheat them! Father, when I find a bride
Love, simple as the dawn, must come to me,
To link us in a life-affinity
Of heart and mind. And she — she must not aim
To sell her birthright for a place or name."

The king turned speechless. Tremblingly he glared
At the rash prince like some vindictive foe
In ominous silence. Then his fury flared
To fire and tempest. "Choose the way you go!
Not mine the failing if this bitter blow
Be fitly punished! In your rooms you'll stay
For seven weeks! We'll guard you night and day!

"Nay, more! It's time your heedless ways be done,
Time that you honor some imperial aim!
And when your long imprisonment ends, my son,
Your follies too must end — and you must name
Some object worthy of your princely fame
And your eventual kingship. Else, I fear,
We'll have to try some treatment more severe."

III

So for long weeks the prince remained confined,
Locked in his gilt and rosewood rooms alone.
Yet empires were explored within his mind,
And he went ranging through the starred unknown,
And hence would never grumble, or bemoan
His scowling fortunes, since he sought the key
To the great secret of man's destiny.

He wondered, as in moody hours before,
Why he was born the scion of a king,
And what the purpose of the life he bore
More than the reason for the wrens that sing
Or pansy-faces briefly gay in spring.
A flash, a flutter, and a laugh or sigh,
And other lives like gnats gyrating by!

"Oh, for a glimpse beyond the utmost veil
Into the fog-rimmed meaning of it all,
Why men, blown cloudlike, balk a scattering gale
Or hammer lifelong at a hidden wall
Till one surmounts it and a thousand fall.
And all for what? Would the poor clown or slave
Slumber more soundly in a sultan's grave?

"And all for what, for what?" With wondering eyes
He questioned the sunlight and the wind and rain.
"Why do bewilderment and sorrow rise
Like April torrents to engulf in pain
The seeking heart? Oh, why? And what the gain?
And whence do towering aspirations spring
As with dim prescience of some deathless thing?

"There must be meaning we have not divined,
Some purpose in the radiance of the rose,
Some light beyond the cloud-peaks, thunder-lined,
And in the spirit's purgatorial throes,
Some gleam of beauty that no mortal knows
But that secretive time may yet unbare
For him with eyes to see and will to dare.

"And may the fortunate seeker not be I?
May I not trace the fire behind the dawn,
Read the red lettering of the twilight sky,
And learn the language of the fern and fawn?
And may my spirit not at last be drawn
Into some lonely height where knowledge lies
Like a blue open plain before my eyes?

"Gladly to this I'd dedicate my days,
Risking my youth where wrinkled deserts spread,
But so escaping those plush-swaddled ways
That close in darkness, with man's heart unfed.
Father, forgive me if the path I tread
Be not your path, for sooner would I die
Than seek no more life's whither, whence, and why."

IV

But how to seek, no less than how to find,
Still was a coiled enigma, for there seemed
To be no answer in the questing mind,
And from the fog-strewn world no answer beamed.
And though he pondered, agonized and dreamed,
The longed-for vision failed him, till one day
Chance, which is fate, appeared to point the way.

Wearying of the long monotony
Of wall-bound life, the prince contrived at last,
By golden gifts, to win the palace key;
And through the portals in the dawn he passed
When guards were few and watched with eyes downcast;
And, mantled grayly in a peasant's gown,
Stole like a beggar to the wakening town.

Across the royal park, and through the woods,
And out along the clattering clayey road
Where ox-teams creaked with bales of jeweled goods
And camels plodded with a human load,
Free as a nomad chief Lodalga strode,
Drawing deep gulps of morning's lucid air,
And whistling like a man with never a care.

And long he hummed a merry tune, and long
Held to the highway, though the heavens blazed;
Then, where a brooklet made melodious song,
He paused to rest while sheep serenely grazed,
And making a song of simple things he praised
The wide, blue mystery of the world, that brings
Joy to the beggar past the joy of kings.

Sprawled on the grass by that meandering stream,
A lanky traveler chose to chat awhile,
A tall gray man with iron eyes a-gleam
And a far light and music in his smile.
His raveled garments said that many a mile
Of road had borne his footprints; and his beard,
Like his dense hair, hung grizzled and unsheared.

He told Lodalga of the golden lands
Close to the sunset border, where the sea
Rolled its long organ blasts on glistening sands
And wild wind-bugles led the symphony,
And smokeless valleys curved, immense and free,
Pine-needled where the long green ridges rose
To the white brilliance of unmelting snows.

"Oh, that I might go roaming lands so fair!"
Lodalga cried, enchanted. "Tell me, friend,
Are not perhaps the secrets hidden there
Of mortal life, the meaning and the end
Of all these sad and querulous days we spend?
Surely, by chartless peaks and unplumbed seas,
One can decipher ageless mysteries!"

"Would that I knew!" the wanderer gravely said.
"But who can know? And yet — there runs a tale
That if you travel steadily ahead
Far over the plain along a sunset trail
To ice-crags battered by the wind and hail,
You may, with fortune, learn the why and how
Of all the riddles that perplex you now.

"High on the loftiest peak of all the range,
In a chill fastness far from human sight,
Walled from the ruinous touch of time and change,
There is a pool that sparkles mirror-bright.
And he who peers in it, and drinks its light,
May catch a phantom gleam, a flash of wings,
And read the plan and purpose of all things."

"Oh, how to find that pool? Oh, stranger, how?"
Pleaded the youth, shaking in ecstasy.
"Answer, where are those mountains? Where? I vow
The eternal secrets must be won by me!"
But the old man nodded dejectedly.
"Be not too sure, my lad! For all we know
There is no pool upon those peaks of snow.

"I too have sought for it – and garnered straw.
I too have trudged the lone, ascending track
Where knife-edged boulders tore me like a saw
And snow-winds swirled and howled and drove me back.
You who are young may have the power I lack
And so may conquer – but I feel at times
That pool is where no mortal ever climbs."

The wanderer, rising, fumbled for his staff.
"O Youth, be not so blind as I!" he said.
"Trail no mirages, lest the heavens laugh!"
And off he shambled with a dragging tread,
While the young prince, a fever in his head,
Slowly retraced his way to court, like one
Whose eyes catch glory from the rising sun.

Part II

THE ESCAPE

I

The vision would not leave him. Days went by
And still he brooded on the wondrous tale
Told by the vagrant: "Surely, I must try
To take the solitary glacial trail
Into the topless crags. What though I fail?
All agonies and dangers must be dared
Before one meets the Ultimate unbared!"

But crippling doubt would lance into his mind.
"Why clutch a guttering flame? Would it not be
Wiser to make my home with humankind
On the warm plain, not spilling life to see
The ice-mirages of eternity?
Perhaps the pool is not upon the peak
But in the valley, where the millions seek."

Yet always some opposing fire shone bright:
"Not so! It's only on the lone snow-stair
One may pursue the vision and the light;
And the elusive pool must glimmer there.
I too shall seek it. Life turns cold and bare
Without the flash of some far-sparkling hope
To draw one, hungering, up the long gray slope."

Often with passion, both in wakeful dreams
And dreams of sleep, the prince would fix his eyes
Far on those mountaintops whose spectral gleams
Hint of the lamps beyond all men's surmise.
"There is my kingdom, where the eagle flies!"
He fervently promised. "I shall go, shall go!
With those blue peaks above, what meaning here below?"

Firm was the purpose that inspired the prince
After his lonely weeks at last were done.
And then King Helmud, hoping to convince
Of full forgiveness, called to see his son.
"Lodalga, your allotted time is run;
You've had your chance to meditate, and plan
A life-course worthy of our royal clan."

"I've planned indeed, O Sire," the youth replied,
"And crave your favor to indulge my whim."
And while the sovereign listened solemn-eyed,
His son, in eloquent speech, acquainted him
With the weird pool upon the mountain's rim.
But Helmud's face was flushed with sullen flame
When he divined the lad's adventurous aim.

"No son of mine shall risk the crags!" he swore.
"A prince's place is on the plains and seas!
And would you, like a moonstruck child, explore
In the moth-quest of shadowy mysteries? —
You, who should rule the State's realities!
Oh, come, my son, renounce this mad romance!
Prepare yourself to swing an emperor's lance!"

"An emperor's lance, my lord, is frail as down
Against the fire that ardent minds ignite.
Oh, I would feel enchained; I'd sink and drown
In the world's stagnant waters, if no bright
And welcoming vision called me to the height.
Circled by cloud-walled peaks of death and fate,
How can I trudge the lowland roads of State?"

Quaking with wrath, the monarch stamped away;
And, striding to the judgment room again,
Summoned a ring of councillors, to say
The prince still scorned the paths of grown-up men.
And all heaved deep and mournful sighs, as when
Battles were lost or legions slain; and all
Declared Lodalga sunk beyond recall —

All except one, the eldest of the band,
Who pleaded, "Youth must blaze its trail! O Sire,
Why be alarmed? Perhaps I understand.
The poor lad burns, and overflows with fire
For that romance which opening hearts require
And that adventure which not seldom leads
To golden conquest and heroic deeds.

"So be not harsh. Grant him his longed-for quest,
And humor thus his hot, full-blooded ways.
What if he quaffs a drink of life? It's best
He too should pay the forfeit all youth pays.
Returning from his wanderings, he will praise
His father's wisdom, and will laugh to scorn
His fledgling follies as a cloak outworn."

"True!" said another. And a long debate
Followed with many a daggered stab and thrust.
Some held the plea arch-treason to the State,
And some proclaimed its purpose only just,
Before the king conceded, "If I must,
I'll yield to madcap youth its fiery crown!
So let the prince disport himself as clown,

"And wander like a maniac through the land,
Till by degrees his roving wits return.
But to protect his name, we'll say he's planned
To fight some far barbarians, and to earn
The glittering tribute that no king may spurn."
And so the sovereign called his son, and bade:
"Make ready; seek your magic pool, my lad,

"And I'll provide a royal retinue,
Camels and slaves, an arrow-bearing guard,
Foodstuffs and chests of gold, to bear with you
So that your journey be not over-hard.
I'll hold you due, unless you're evil-starred,
Back at our court within a year or less,
Bearing rich trophies from the wilderness."

"Not that, O father!" cried the prince, amazed.
"I crave no trophies — silk or precious stone.
I burn for wealth no merchant has appraised,
The shadowy undiscovered and unknown,
And if I find it, I must seek alone.
Deem me no ingrate, but I must be free —
Your generous offering would shackle me."

"A madman's raving!" roared the king in wrath.
"Some devil prods you with a venomous goad!
What! would you stoop to walk the common path,
And nudge the brigands of the common road,
And bathe your feet in some rude slave's abode?
Why, one would almost think you scorned your birth
And spat upon your princely pride and worth!

"So if you cannot make the pilgrimage
Cushioned in crimson, make it not at all!
Truly my meanest chambermaid or page
Is more in tune where palace bugles call.
O son, why must you turn my life to gall?
Back to your rooms! There by yourself you'll stay,
With leisure to repent your faults, and pray!"

II

Once more, beneath a stonier new restraint,
Lodalga paced his silken jail alone.
But still he bore the trial without complaint
Or suppliant's murmurs that he would atone.
Defiant, he thought, "Let others have the throne.
My only crown, my citadel shall be
High on the peaks that face eternity."

And now the longing for the mountaintop
And far adventure, raged with mastering power.
By a long knotted rope he made the drop
Out of his prison at the midnight hour,
And, lithely swinging from the black-walled tower,
He reached the pickets of the palace gate
Where sabred sentries, nodding, lay in wait.

Mute as a shadow in the moonless dark,
He passed the drowsy guard, and made his way
Over the wall, out of the royal park,
Into the town, where pestilent alleys lay,
And mazy forsaken lanes. When morning's gray
Blinked wanly in the east, ten thousand paces
Sundered the fleeing prince from princely places.

At dawn he paused, traded his purple gown
For peasant's homespun, pennies, salt and bread,
And clad in hempen cloak of dusty brown,
With pighide boots, and veiled and turbaned head,
And shirt all patched with ragged green and red,
The prince resumed his course, with little doubt
The king's militia could not search him out.

Even so, he feared them. Time on time he saw
Helmeted warriors pressing hotly by
With snarls and questions. But he would withdraw
Deep in a thicket, safe from ear and eye,
And listen to some peasant's scared reply
That none in purple robes or princely crown
Passed on this highway from the royal town.

He felt like one who freshly learns to live,
One born in fetters, who at last is free.
Only as vagabond and fugitive
Could he absorb the blue world's majesty.
"I never knew such loveliness could be!"
He cried, enchanted. "One is most a king
Where the bold gale drives past and waters sing!"

Such were the thoughts that moved him many a day,
With the wide blooming earth spread far before.
Into the setting sun he held his way
Over the billowy prairie's boundless floor.
Sometimes he feasted at a plowman's door,
Sometimes he earned his pottage with the hoe,
Sometimes he hungered, and his hopes ran low;

Sometimes he plunged where thundering Augusts weep,
Huddling in mouldy stables from the rain.
Often he forded rivers, or would creep,
Shrivelled with thirst, across a desert plain,
Or thresh his way through armies of daggered cane,
Or in some bouldery gulch or caverned glen
Stare in the steely eyes of highwaymen.

But always, though his limbs grew lean and sore
With questing, questing on the endless road,
He longed for some high cloudy corridor
And scarcely knew he sagged beneath a load.
Driven incessantly as by a goad,
He dreamt of mountains, still befogged from view,
Where haunted pools imaged the heaven's blue.

Many a time, beside some friendly fire,
Or tramping down a rock-scarred windy way
With passing vagabonds, he would inquire
Where the white ranges of his vision lay.
But men would only gasp, and some would say,
"May the gods tell us where those summits are!
Weird as the moon they shine, and not less far!"

Weird as the moon they seemed! How few, how few
Spoke of the pool upon the sprakling height!
Only one man, one gnarled old wanderer, knew
The tale of how it glimmered crystal-bright.
But even he had never reached its site;
And where it was he could not say, nor guess
In what remote and glacial wilderness.

So the worn rover, lifting tired eyes
Where sorrow sang her lonely old refrain,
Would feel his own stark isolation rise,
Almost a living thing, a visible pain,
To ask the meaning of the toil and strain
Upon dark highways, snatching pauper's fare,
With neither earth nor sky nor man to care.

Along the brink of thunder-throated streams,
Or from the watchtower of some starry hill,
Or when the moonlight cast seductive beams
Over a forest lake, and all was still
As though a weird enchanter worked his will,
Often the youth would silently bemoan
That the long journey must be made alone.

And most of all, when loitering in a town
Where ox-teams rattled through a bannered street
And shouting youths, with festal leaves and crown
Bedecked their queen, Lodalga's eyes would greet
Some maiden's ringleted face that shone as sweet
As love itself, the more since life denied
A dear companion wandering at his side.

"With one to share my fortunes," he would say,
"Far easier might I gain the snow-fringed west."
And then again, "Alas, there is no way
Save of the friendless trail and lonely quest."
And on and on and ever on he pressed;
And on and on, still slave beneath the prod
Of that bright vision ruling like a god.

Wrinkling his brow, did he not sometimes grieve
For vast dominions recklessly tossed aside,
And in slow midnights, hunger to retrieve
His princely purple, and to doff his pride
And hasten back to court, and claim as bride
Whoever King Helmud favored, and prepare
For those gold-broidered robes that sovereigns wear?

If doubt tormented him and fear assailed
(And who that's human can escape their sting?),
His purpose, blown and storm-tossed, never failed;
His eyes, however weary, would not cling
To sunned horizons that were vanishing.
Indomitably forward he would gaze
Where further skylines met the earth in haze.

But not until the leaden-footed weeks
Had lengthened to a year did he obtain
Faint intimation that the fabled peaks
Were not cloud-vapors, and his purpose vain.
Then, dimly banked above the distant plain,
Mistily blue beneath the evening skies,
He saw the pronged and horny mountains rise.

At first, amid the gathering mauve and gray
Of phantom twilight, those far ranges seemed
Less like the solid, stony hills of day
Than fairy mountains that an artist dreamed.
But when the clear, prosaic morning beamed
Over the wild plateau, he still could see
Pale ridges shouldering to infinity —

Ridges that bade him, "Match the antelope's pace
And bound across the undulant fields between!
Do battle with the pinnacles face to face,
And in some tangly forest or ravine
Or where bald glaciers throw a deathly spell,
Grasp at immortal secrets long unseen
And fathom truths no living lips could tell!"

Over the plain, whose unfrequented road
Had dwindled to a winding, stubbly track
Where gray wolves slunk, the lone adventurer strode,
Worn by his seeking, wearied by his pack,
But never pausing till the night stared black
Into his yearning face, and he might lie
In dream-tossed sleep till dawn had fired the sky.

Always, in sunlit hours, Lodalga's gaze
Would travel, searching, to the rim of sight,
Where, streaked by cloud or red in sunset's blaze,
With vests and jackets of enameled white
And pyramidal flanks of Alpine height,
The ranges, cloven in an axe-head band,
Seemed the mad carvings of a giant hand.

Then what exhilaration spurred the prince,
As of a wanderer from a foreign shore
Who sees home places, lost to mind long since,
Yet throwing wide a long-neglected door
Back to a life abandoned years before!
And as the peaks loomed nearer, they became
Like old companions he might now reclaim.

Oh, to surmount those summoning cliffs of snow,
To stand, chest forward, on the topmost peak,
Stare in the world-reflecting pool, and know
One saw the light which all, unconscious, seek,
And reached the bourn whereto all men must go!
Soon, soon — so blazed the wanderer's sudden hope —
He might toil, conquering, up the last white slope!

Part III

THE SHEPHERDESS OF THE PLAINS

I

And then new pits and gorges crossed his track.
Almost at arm-length of the foothill range
Fate, striking like a dagger in the back,
Opened a drama, desperate and strange.
His limbs were shaken by a torturing change:
He wavered, stumbled, like a man grown old;
By turns he sweltered and was shivering cold;

His heart gave hammer thumps; his forehead ached
And flushed a bloody crimson, while his breast
Pained dully, and his thirst could not be slaked.
Feebly he tottered, still into the west,
And time on time he had to pause and rest,
But always found he bore a heavier load
When he must tread again the hard, long road.

A shepherd maiden, when the night drew near
And flocks were driven homeward, stood amazed
To see a tall and staggering rover veer
Round the road's bend, as though age-worn and dazed.
And as, in mute bewilderment, she gazed,
The lean shape trembled in a palsying spell,
Swayed like a warrior arrow-struck, and fell.

Muffling a cry, she dashed on nimble feet
Straight to the stricken stranger, and began
To warm his pallid figure, and entreat
The unwilling life-stream of the lifeless man
Back to the limbs where icy slow it ran.
And while her fingers, like swift shuttles, plied,
She saw how youthful-fair he was, and sighed.

And he, when through the darkness where he lay,
The light in pale confusion broke anew,
Marvelled to see two eyes of cornflower blue
Staring in wonder mixed with vague dismay —
And marvelled more to hear the maiden say,
"Traveler, be not distressed. Feel no alarm.
We'll care for you, and shelter you from harm."

Dimly it came to him that he had died
And in some lovelier kingdom was reborn,
Where feathered angels floated at his side
And lonely wanderers were not left forlorn
To push, with bleeding hands, through rock and thorn.
And she with tearful pity in her eyes —
Was she a watcher out of Paradise?

The vision faded out. A withering fire
Again devoured him, and his brain grew numb.
He did not see the moist-cheeked maid retire
And call two kinsmen, who made haste to come,
And finding him in wild delirium,
Lifted him gently, carried him straightway
To their rude low-walled house of thatch and clay.

II

There for slow weeks he lingered, fever-racked,
With cheeks deep-sunken, and dull burning head,
Speechless with agony. And yet he lacked
No homely care. All day, beside his bed,
The maiden Lanya plied her wheel and thread,
But ready, at a gesture, to attend
With herbs and drink, and be his nurse and friend.

And sometimes, when he slumbered, and his face,
Averted, seemed to stare at worlds remote,
Her eyes, soft-smiling at the lad, would trace
The chiselled contours of his mouth and throat;
And with a glance half-wistful she would note
The imperial sweep of forehead, and the hair
Flaxen and light as fabled mermen wear.

After the days and endless weary days
And nights of tortured dream, there came an hour
When the pale youth could smile on her, and praise
Her dimpled cheek, her charm and healing power.
Then benedictions in a grateful shower
Poured from his lips; and her slim head withdrew
To hide the blush at hidden truths it knew.

And now, while spinning, she would gaze at him,
Holding him dazzled by her lyric eyes.
And sometimes, briefly, his own eyes grew dim
As when one peers at new-discovered skies
Where Jupiters and strange ringed Saturns rise.
And constellations, undiscerned before,
Gleamed through the opening in a cloudy door.

Oh, what new glowing ecstasy was this
That, hotter than the fever, stirred his brain
With daylong dreams of overmastering bliss,
Visions of wonder, and heart-wrenching pain,
Till longing held unconquerably its reign
Over his life, and he perceived no god
Save for a reverenced girlish smile or nod?

Where now the hunger for the upland trail,
The long, lone climb, the pool upon the peak?
What could his months of suffering toil avail
When in a shepherd's hut he lay, too weak
To face an assailant wind, to dare or seek?
Why not renounce old glittering bubble quests
And take the wealth of opening treasure chests?

Thus, when returning strength restored his world,
He pondered, fogged amid perplexities.
By life, the Janus-headed, he was hurled
Between the jaws of two opposed decrees:
Yonder the old magnetic mysteries
Of ice-browed mountains; here a sparkling glance
Lovely and bright with all a life's romance.

Yet he must rise again, again pursue
The friendless spiral of his destiny,
And climb sheer ridges where each breath he drew
Hurt like a knife-edge turning cruelly.
And let no honeyed call, no witchery
Of hands or lips allure him to a net
Tangled for failure and a spined regret.

Alas, a plan far harder than he knew!
When, slowly convalescing, he would sit,
Observing Lanya skillfully weave, or brew
Some healing lotion, or sedately knit,
He found, distracted, he had not the wit
To thwart her smiles, or wield a battle lance
Against the entrapping legions of her glance.

For hours the two would talk; he'd hear her tell
Of how, a shepherd's daughter, she had known
Only the plains, obliged for life to dwell
On treeless ranges scarred by briars and stone;
And how, when rambling through the fields alone
Hunting lost sheep, she had whole days to ponder
What lay beyond the blue horizon yonder.

And he, in luminous hues, described far lands
Where kings made merry in a crystal hall,
And sometimes, while his fingers took her hands,
With reminiscent eyes he would recall
The rainbow pageant and the painted ball.
But these he pictured with a cool disdain,
As less than any open peak or plain.

And when at last, with slow, irregular gait,
He walked again beneath the blowing sky,
And she, like the bland image of his fate,
Stood at his elbow, ready to supply
All that he beckoned with a word or sigh —
Then tenderly he would confide to her
How good the ways of maids and shepherds were.

Under the night-skies, when the stars burned clear
Across a universe of shadowy grass,
He poured those special sweets into her ear
That many a lad has murmured to a lass
In the dear haunted hours that gleam and pass.
And she, eyes glistening in the dark above,
Spoke the fond message of her youth and love.

And all the whispered vows and happy tears,
Impulsive fondlings and contented sighs,
The joy and heartthrobs of ten thousand years
Of men and maidens, came as by surprise
To fill their world, and make their spirits wise
In that great law which rules like song, and brings
More power to stars and moonlight than to kings.

Back to the cottage, slowly, arm in arm,
Speechless as ghosts, down the still night they strayed,
Like spellbound wanderers warded from all harm
By Merlin's mantle or a genie's blade.
Yet even then some treacherous thought betrayed
Lodalga's gladness — wilful fancy showed
A dim pool glittering on a mountain road.

And he was led, with words of fire, to speak
Of fabled ranges luminously white,
And ancient mysteries, guarded by the peak,
Which lured him, lured him like a signal light,
Into the darkness, up the rocky height.
And then, new passion in his quavering tone,
He pleaded, "Let me not go forth alone!

"But come, belovèd, come and climb with me
Into the sunset mountains, where the snows
Veil the key secrets of our destiny,
And wait, in ageless silence, to disclose
Wonders that all men seek but no man knows.
Oh, come, belovèd — let our youth take wing
Beyond the dust of every earthly thing.

"Let us go soaring, eagle-like and blest,
Over the snow-peaks of the ultimate land,
Where, in long vistas glimmering to the west,
Infinity shines bright, and we may stand
On the world's houseless summit, hand in hand,
And, fused together, see beyond the line
Of the gray horizon and the starred divine.

"Belovèd, come," he urged. "Come far away
Into those mapless highlands, airy clear,
Where all the trials and tragedies that slay,
The wounds that shatter, fade and disappear."
But she, with breast soft-heaving, seemed to hear
Scarcely a word he uttered; and a sigh
Came as her earliest, undesigned reply.

"You tell of wanderings I shall never know,
And heights I cannot reach," she made lament.
"For I am daughter of the plains, and so
Would only perish in the bold ascent.
Gladly I'd follow, follow where you went,
And yet my weight would be a weary drag
To bind your limbs, and make your spirit lag."

The silence closed around them once again,
And the chill stars looked down in bitter mirth.
A night-beast grumbled from some lonely den,
And night-winds howled, and shadows cloaked the earth.
Then on his lips tempestuous speech had birth,
Shaking him with a quick unreasoned fear
Lest he relinquish all he held most dear.

"When I was dying, you were kind," he cried,
"And nursed me back to palpitant life once more.
And if my famishing spirit failed and died,
Would you but hear me call — and close the door?
Oh, if I roamed without you, how ignore
These sad, sweet hours? Always I should see
Your shadow like a phantom mocking me.

"And every wind would breathe aloud your name,
And every rivulet murmur songs of you.
And you would haunt the sunset's tragic flame,
And the cold fogs of night, and morning dew.
Wherever I wander, you must wander too!
Leave your safe walls, my Lanya! Come, and take
The mountain trail for love's immortal sake!"

Tears were her answer — stormy tears fast turning
To words as hot and desperate as his own.
"Remain, my lover! Let no rainbow yearning
Dazzle you, moth-like, to embark alone
From the calm ranges of the dear and known
Into the dark and perilous. Stay with me!
Stay, and you'll learn how happy we shall be!

"Oh, you shall find the light of common things
Fairer than gilds the glacier's fleshless dome!
Stay! — walk the fields, and taste the joy that springs
From bees and daisies and the doors of home!
Over the wide sheep-pastures let us roam,
Scorning the buttes and crags! True lovers crave
Some ampler housing than a rock or cave!"

Bright longing, as she pleaded, lit her face,
And her dim tresses, in a fluttering trail,
Wavered like shadows in the wakening gale;
And her slim figure had the ease and grace
Of some pure spirit, free from earth's embrace.
And a sudden storm convulsed Lodalga's heart
With many a brooding cloud and lightning dart;

And he was borne on some torrential stream,
While on the bank, with gesturing hands outspread,
She watched him sinking, sinking; and the gleam
Of her moist eyes might charm him from the dead
Back to the world, if only he would be led;
And when she beckoned, he would hear no more
The whirling, strangling waters hiss and roar.

Then he was fired to draw her back again
Into his arms, and never let her go,
And there forget the world of winds and men,
The empty highway, and the peaks of snow,
And with her love abide content below
In the green valley, and no longer clutch
At starbeams that receded at a touch.

Suddenly, with a moan, a stifled cry,
He seized her hands; and their long-drawn embrace
Cancelled the meadows and the stars and sky,
And left two bodiless beings in their place.
But some unspoken torment racked his face
When he released her, and his eyes took flame
With kindling of an agonizing aim.

And, standing just beside her in the dark,
With close-pressed fingers but averted sight,
He painfully poured out words that quenched the spark
Starring her eyes, and quelled an inner light:
"Belovèd, even as the birds in flight,
I seek the clouds — and if your native plain
Must hold you fettered, I cannot remain.

Farewell, belovèd! I am called to go
Down the long road where last horizons shine.
Such is my fate! But I'll return, I know,
When I have pierced the mountain's hidden shrine
And looked upon the timeless and divine.
I shall return! So do not sigh or grieve.
When next I come to you, I shall not leave!"

"You leave forever!" With beseeching eyes
Yet with proud anger shuddering in her voice,
She hurled her challenge. "Love neglected, dies!
And when you choose, you make eternal choice!
Choose, then, my lover! Let us both rejoice
If you are blest — but do not go away
And think new seasons will restore today.

"The very stars shall alter in their track,
These blossomy fields shall not allure as now,
But clouds shall gather ere you wander back,
And we shall meet as strangers, marvelling how
We ever shared a passionate kiss or vow.
Oh, do not leave me! How shall love stay green
When years, like ghostly hand-marks, stare between?

Then her tense fingers clutched his mantle's hem,
And her imploring face shone with a light
Of witchery beyond his power to stem,
That made him all but captive to its might.
And under the sparkle of the spellbound night
And in the enthrallment of her eloquent glance,
He seemed to own no mistress but romance . . .

Until again blunt reason gave him words:
"Since the heights call me, let them call me soon!
Here on the plain, amid the drowsy herds,
Where the rank grass confronts a wastrel moon,
I should but find my spirit out of tune
With the whole world, and daily should lament
That life denied one dearly sought event.

"And you, boon comrade in my grief, would learn
That I was mated to the Might-Have-Been;
And, all the desolate years, my thoughts would turn
Sadly to those high peaks I hoped to win.
So let us not commit the crowning sin
Against the days to be. Farewell! Farewell!
Long I shall dream of you wherever I may dwell!"

For the last time, the girl was folded round
In quivering arms that she would feel no more . . .
Till, like a shadow, almost without sound,
He slipped away, and left her at her door,
While grayly, on the prairie's eastern shore,
The sad dawn broke; and one long, muffled cry
Sobbed to the lonely fields, and moaned without reply.

Part IV

THE POOL UPON THE PEAK

I

Among the ice-beaked mountains to the west
Of Helmud's kingdom, where the spires of snow
Surmount the cloud-spires, pendent crest on crest,
And crab-armed canyons ramble worlds below,
Sometimes the sleet-wind and the rain would blow
Round a slim traveler who traced alone
The snake-meanderings of a trail of stone.

Stray huntsmen saw him on some luminous height,
A black form etched against the sunset red,
And shepherds in the valley would invite
The fire-eyed rover to a crust or bed.
And where the spark-girt nomad tents were spread
By cliffs and torrents, men would watch him roam
Like a lost phantom mourning hope and home.

Wolf-threaded forests knew him, where the boughs
Gave noon a roof of twilight; he would toil
Up rock-piled summits, with a cave for house,
When spitting geysers would seethe, and fountains boil
Beneath scrub pines that sucked a beggared soil;
And in green bouldery gorges he would wander
Where twisted streams poured with the crash of thunder.

Lonely, forever lonely! — none could say
That he had ever held a comrade's hand.
And some who, unobserved, had seen him stray
Up the gnarled slopes, and over wind-blown sand,
Thorn-brush and cactus of a thirsty land,
Rumored his eyes had some unearthly gleam,
As though his sole companion were a dream.

And strange the tales that whisperers told of him
Beside the campfire or the tavern gate:
Wearing a tangly beard, and bronzed of limb,
He had the manners of the proud and great,
And spoke as one bred to a lord's estate;
And, in his slumber, he'd been heard to moan
And mutter furious things about a throne.

"A hundred peaks," one grizzled rover swore,
"Have seen him scale stone ledges, yard on yard
To the raw summits; and a hundred more
Have watched him where the cleft plateau is scarred.
Never he pauses though the way is hard,
For still, far-off — or so the wise men think —
A magic pool shines on the mountain's brink."

But others, listening to the tale, would smile
And say the pool shone in the windy air.
And, laughing at the madman, they would while
The hours away; and prattling tongues would share
The jests and raillery at a joke so rare . . .
And thus five years went by . . . And all that time
The wanderer had not ceased to search and climb.

II

When the fifth summer had recalled the snows
From the high valleys, laying rugs of grass,
The lonely seeker was observed to pass
Where Kungla's magisterial peak arose
Like an ice-god — how tall no mortal knows.
And there, amid the furthest, whitest range,
Lodalga prayed his barren fate would change.

For life had struck him with a tiger-claw
And slashed the sinews of his doughtiest hope.
And he was not the youth who, years before,
Had dreamt of triumph and rejoiced to cope
With giants on the boulder-bastioned slope.
But the dark traceries of his brooding face
Showed proof of suffering time could not erase.

And some that knew him in a happier year
Might now had passed him by without a nod.
The wolfskin mantle of the mountaineer,
The rough spiked boots, the pack and oaken rod,
Scarcely befitted one revered as god
By a great kingdom; while his uncropped hair
Hung scraggly as the forelocks of a bear.

And yet, when peering deep into those eyes
Aglow with sad, impenetrable fire,
One might behold fresh beauty, and surmise
The strength that springs of unfulfilled desire
When the bold soul takes courage to aspire
Above the walls that bound it. So the youth,
Unknowing, bore the first impress of truth.

But inklings of the madness of despair
Shuddered across the sun-tanned wistful face
When tortuously down a craggy stair
He crawled, and stood at towering Kungla's base.
He thought how many a freezing mountain place
Had seen him toil as now; how many a time
Hope gave him heart and muscle for the climb;

How always, when his eyes surveyed the peak,
Delusive faith proclaimed that here at last
Glittered the pool he came so far to seek;
Yet how, when every challenged ridge was past
And the ranges rolled beneath him, ocean-vast,
He only viewed bare mountains, wall on wall,
And never saw the longed-for pool at all.

And now, so often were his dreams deceived,
He dared not hope, but took the ascending track
Not as in earlier years, when he believed
In certain conquest at the next attack,
But as a man who brooks no turning back
When once his heart is given, though he die
With parched limbs sprawled beneath a desert sky.

Again to take the coiling, rock-paved trail,
Again to trudge with bleeding hands and knees
Up wet escarpments, where a battering gale
Lunges and cuts with screeching mockeries;
While, like a taunting fate above, one sees
The sky-hung cone, whose haughty blue or gray
Seems, on a slow approach, to slowly draw away.

CANISIUS COLLEGE LIBRARY
BUFFALO, N. Y.

Three suns had sunk in fire, while twinkling night
Kindled her starry lanterns in the dark,
Before the wanderer, with unclouded sight,
Looked on the turrets of his snow-crowned mark.
Then, tapering high above him, straight and white,
He saw the pyramid of the summit rise
To the azure hollow of the pale cold skies.

Grimly he struggled on, for he had seen
No magic pool, though many a loud cascade
Resounded in the forest-robed ravine
And many a foaming rivulet plunged and played.
Nor did he hold that when the climb was made
His searching vision would at last explore
Better than stone and snow-banks, as before.

And yet another night he pitched his camp
On a chill flat above the timber line.
Tossing with only moonlight for a lamp,
He heard the homeless storm-wind sob and whine.
And when the weary dawn began to shine
He took his pack once more, resolved to tread
The peak itself before the west turned red.

Along the precipice's beetling face
He crept with hands that, fly-like, clutched the rock,
When one misstep might hurtle him through space
To a still land where mountains could not mock.
Over torn slopes that glaciers tried to block
And through dim twining passes still he pressed
With eyes firm-fastened on the summoning crest.

The Pool Upon the Peak 53

Then, when the dismal day was nearly done,
He scaled the cliff-walls to a weird plateau,
Whose narrow floor, beneath the yellowing sun,
Bristled with ice that shed a steely glow.
And on its further reaches, just below
The spearhead peak, Lodalga paused to view
A tiny oval lake of glimmering blue.

A haunted blue! the blue of watchful eyes
Grave with the soul's unfathomable light.
Slowly, discolored by the darkening skies,
It paled to gray, then turned carnelian-bright
With the reflected altar-fires of night.
And in its tranquil face one might behold
The peak, the burning heavens, and clouds of gold.

And as Lodalga watched, the sunset waned
With far-strewn ashes glaring anvil-red.
Soon, on the waveless waters, there remained
Only a blush, an afterglow that shed
Ghost-glimmers from the radiance overhead,
Then faded like a mist, till not one spark
Pierced the engulfing mantle of the dark.

And now the stars looked out, and on the lake
The youth beheld their mirrored splendor shine.
He saw the light of lonely Venus break
Along the surface in a glistening line,
As though it cut a path to lands divine,
And called him from the worn world's stormy shore
To where still waters shone forevermore.

In silence stronger than tumultous sound
The charmed plateau and shadowy mountains lay.
Slowly, as over consecrated ground,
The cautious breezes moved; and far away,
Above the peak, the ridges' phantom gray,
Some noiseless meteor now and then would gleam
Like the last dying embers of a dream.

And all the long and frosty hours of night,
While the far-circling stars went faintly past,
He searched the dim lake-ripples for a light
Only one lake in all the world could cast.
Here, surely, was the magic pool at last!
But why no wafture of the silvery wings
Bright with a halo of immortal things?

Only the constellations, darkly turning!
Only the dusky peak and phantom sky!
Oh, where deliverance from the ache, the yearning
That led him like a lamp-drawn summer fly?
Was there but this, and then the call to die? —
Cold ranges, and the night-time, and the stars
Held in lone pools no human shadow mars?

While still he pondered and the half-moon peeped
From a torn skyline swathed in copper mist,
And spilt a spectral flame where snow was heaped
And lit the water with pale amethyst,
It seemed that some celestial exorcist
Conjured the shades away, and called a shape
Star-brilliant, in a white archangel's cape.

Perhaps it was not with his eyes he saw
But with a deeper seeing of the mind.
For as he watched the giant shape withdraw
It beckoned to the pool, and then declined
Swift as the sunlight when a man goes blind.
And weirdly, as it faded, came the thought
Now he might look upon the goal he sought.

Soon, in the water, burnished sunrise shone
With bright reflections of a heavenly fire,
And from the crimson-clouded twilight zone
He seemed to hear the seraphs chant in choir
And felt himself, with eyes upraised, aspire
In consecration to that luminous height
Gold-ceilinged with the day's awakening light.

Then, with the throb of one who first descries
Headlands and bays of some uncharted shore,
He gave a low, short murmur of surprise,
Shaken by ecstasies unfelt before.
Strangely, as when an iron-bolted door
Swings open, and far-twinkling vistas smile
Of turquoise sea, blue cliff, or azure isle —

So strangely, in a vision, he was drawn
Out of the mist in which he groped in pain
Into a radiant upland where the dawn
Made every hill and meadow picture-plain.
No more he need go fumbling to attain
The pool-hid secret — at his feet it shone
Brightly as truth that he had always known.

And in the blazing funeral-pyre of day
Kindling the lonely waters; in the sweep
Of constellations whose arcane array
Circled the desert of the midnight deep;
And in the dawn, whose wandering eye would peep
Life-granting through drab cloud, Lodalga read
The mysteries of the living and the dead;

The mysteries of the heavens and the earth,
And all that was, all moments yet to be,
And those strange shadows gathering round our birth
That point, through rainy grief or roselip mirth,
To the last gateway . . . and a shrouded Sea.
And viewing what no tongue could ever tell,
Lodalga stood as in a sorcerer's spell.

The cycle of the planets drifting, drifting
Across the borderless waste-land of the sky,
The light of suns submerged but newly lifting,
And light of stars that change but never die —
In these the secret of all things must lie,
And these are imaged, as on fog-blurred glass,
In glints and flickerings of the lives we pass.

All the fixed movement and the slow progression
From light to dark, and back from dark to light,
While hope and fear and love in long succession
Color men's seasons in their firefly flight;
All the weird heavens, closed to human sight,
And that grave flux and flow which seems to draw
Sun-swarms and satellites in age-old law —

These must be seen and known before one knows
The meaning hidden at the heart of time;
But these are only clear to him who goes
Bleeding and footsore up those stairs that climb
To the forsaken peaks; and all the grime,
The din and dust of man's affairs must fade
Before the immortal truths may be displayed.

So mused Lodalga as he stared in awe
At pallid waters rippling elfin blue,
Making him oddly part of all he saw,
Merging his being in the mirrored view
Of peak and sky, until he scarcely knew
If the great world lay spread beyond, or he
Contained the ages and infinity.

Illuminations, fitful as the light
And interlacing shadow when the gale
Ruffles thin leafage, raised him to a height
That made tall mountains level with the vale,
And made his wanderings seem a pygmy's tale,
And touched his mind with some eternal lore
That lips may not disclose nor eyes explore.

And yet he felt the joy not all his own
At truth pulsating in his heart like song.
Faintly he heard some plaintive overtone
So reminiscent of the wall-bound throng
And all the lightning thrusts of pain and wrong
In the world's darkness, that he throbbed to show
His revelation to the hosts below.

He longed to glide away on wingéd feet
Back to the towns where thousands swarmed and died,
And lead the sufferers from the fuming street
To the long silence of the mountainside
And the charmed pool, and there with them abide
Forever! — so delivering all mankind
From the hard roads they followed, maimed and blind,

And so restoring in gray-windowed souls
The torch that lights the rainbow and the star,
And piercing with its rays high clouded goals
And summoning through the fog to peaks afar.
"O men, who on some unseen granite bar
Beat out your lives in vain, come, follow me,
Follow!" Lodalga cried in ecstasy,

"And you shall know, as I, the immortal dream
Where still lakes, brooding, look at lonely skies,
And in your hearts a guardian light shall gleam
To flash a glimpse of hidden paradise
And tell what barren fury underlies
The highway and the court. Oh, come, and learn
The truth for which the questing ages burn!

"And so, above your sad and wandering lives
Let some unfading signal-lantern shine,
That even though old heartache still survives,
You may not languish, since you'll have a sign
Hinting of ends undying and divine.
O unseen friends, down to the vale I go
That you may climb and learn the truths I know!"

Then, with a final, lingering, awesome glance
At the blue pool and scarcely bluer skies,
He started slowly, still as in a trance,
Down a long rocky saddle; and his eyes
Turned with a mystic's vision-held surmise
Far, far away, beyond the last dim peak
Where spread the misty plain that he once more would seek.

Part V

THE RETURN

I

Five years went by — slow-footed, weary years
Laden with bitter-sweet of joy and pain
For swarms that trod, in ecstasy or tears,
The level highways of the town and plain.
And babes were born, and grizzled lords were slain,
And youths were lovesick, and a million men
Struggled and dreamed, and sank to rise again.

But there was one who in the toil and hopes
Of sweaty myriads, played an alien part.
Sad as a dungeoned emperor who gropes
Round dusky doors and gratings, he would start
Over the fields or through the muttering mart,
Seeking a prince or slave to lend an ear
To frenzied words that few desired to hear.

Men called him mad — and surely there was madness
In cheeks that long, crisscrossing furrows marred,
Eyes that were dim with everlasting sadness
And sun-browned countenance dried and weather-scarred,
As of a wanderer old and evil-starred;
And that dense beard, in straggly disarray,
Whose unshorn bristles showed a fringe of gray.

Men called him mad — and always mocking laughter
Rang in his footsteps. In the farm or town
Stray urchins, shouting jeers, would follow after,
And armed with clods and mire, would hunt him down.
And when he spoke, good citizens would frown
And mumble oaths and curses; some demanded
That for his crimes he be impaled or branded.

But though a thousand arms were raised to smite
And sullen eyes would flash derisive fire,
His gaze was fastened still upon that light
Marking the apex of his life's desire,
But which the swarms who gave their days for hire
Could never see, or, seeing, could not know —
Blind ants oblivious of the starlight's glow.

For the sad years had taught him, more and more,
That what he viewed he had to view alone;
And he no longer fancied all men bore
Radiant aims, and transports like his own,
Or longed for doorways into worlds unknown,
Or saw this earth with vision fixed above
The walls that held them like a squeezing glove.

Often he thought of how, when first he hastened
Down from the pool where timeless secrets lay,
He pleaded, with calm spirit still unchastened,
"Pursue, O friends, the eternal mountain way!"
But found, in disenchantment and dismay,
Crowds of his hearers would but gape and glare,
Till titters and guffaws would fill the air.

And of the thousands who had heard him speak
And caught a spark from his impassioned eyes,
Not one had ever looked upon the peak
Or answered save with promises and sighs.
Not one! and he was waxing sadly wise,
Sorrowing less for his own lamp burnt low
Than at discerning no responsive glow.

Still, where untrodden peaks lay cold and bare,
Shone the blue fires of eternity.
And, knowing no enchanter could prepare
Magic instructing shuttered eyes to see,
He felt as lonely as a soul could be —
Lonely to gaze in uncompanioned awe
On mysteries no fellow mortal saw.

And still he viewed the secret light of stars
And silvery watch-fires of the rising day
Beyond the ultimate mountain's rocky bars
Where sky-revealing waveless waters lay.
And in blind snowstorms, in the rains of May
And autumn mist, the vision would revive
And lend him power to hope and will to strive.

But as the years groaned by, and time renewed
The grimacing world's derision and disdain,
It seemed the illumining glimmers he had wooed
Grew more remote; he scarcely could regain
The old resplendence here upon the plain
And in the screeching town. He was as one
Grown blind, who muses on June's vanished sun.

In place of life so vain and fever-racked,
He might have plucked a laurel leaf and crown,
And won the love and reverence that he lacked,
And seen whole empires cringe beneath his frown.
And was it better to be branded clown?
Better to be despised, or mauled and burned
In giving men the enchanted rays they spurned?

A happier man and wiser far than he
Never might leave the lowland dust and mire,
But wade neck-deep in purple revelry
Or seek the love and labor men require
When plagued by no illusive starry fire.
What though he once had glimpsed a heavenly light?
Meteor-brief it shone — and, after that, the night.

Meteor-brief it shone — and what the gain
To groping millions he had sought to bless?
They still would grope, and not forsake the plain
Because weird lanterns in the wilderness
Glittered with brilliance they could never guess.
Oh, why persuade them to the rash ascent
When in the valley fog they crept content?

So, in bleak hours, the wanderer made complaint,
When men were cruel and skies hung gray and stern.
But though he faltered and his zeal turned faint,
Always old exaltations would return,
And once again, young-hearted, he would burn
To kindle fires that summoned all mankind
To the far peak where knowledge lay enshrined.

II

And now ten years had faded since he fled,
Too sanguine-tempered, from King Helmud's court.
And in the rude, adventurous life he led
Only a rare and long-relayed report
Described his royal father; how he sought
Ramparts of power, ruled with iron claws
And swung the sword in vain, victorious wars.

But time had personal tidings to disclose.
One winter night the roving prince had found
Brief refuge from the charging, dizzying snows
Beside a tavern fire, amid the sound
Of roistering laughter roaring all around;
And while he stared into the fitful flame
He gave a start . . . he heard his father's name.

"Alas for Helmud!" came a muffled sigh.
"Alas, our realm has fallen on evil days!"
And as Lodalga stared, he heard reply,
"I fear the fates conspire, with devils' ways,
And vanquish one too nobly proud for praise.
Not in a thousand years the gods will bring
An abler warrior or a wiser king!"

"Not in a thousand years," another said,
"Such majesty and might will grace the land!"
And, hearing in a spasm of grief and dread,
Lodalga, with a hot and trembling hand,
Halted the speaker. "Tell me more!" he cried
In tones that thundered like a lord's command.
"Surely, you did not say King Helmud died!"

All eyes were fixed upon Lodalga now,
And tipsy revelers crowded close to hear.
"Helmud still lives; yet couriers tell us how
He pines, and has not left his couch this year,
But groans tormented orders for his bier.
And in the court and royal town men pray
To stay that hand no prayer can ever stay.

"What fire devours his body no man knows —
A hundred wizards have invoked their art,
And still he sickens; some believe his woes
Knock at the secret chambers of his heart.
Ten years ago the affliction had its start
When that demented youth, the eldest prince,
Vanished on roads where none have trailed him since.

"You know how furious was our monarch's grief:
How broiling fever burnt into his brain,
Until the pitying years had lent relief
And men supposed he had forgot his pain.
But there are memories that will not be slain,
And so King Helmud, as the dark draws near,
Harkens a voice he cannot choose but hear.

"And sometimes, in the slow, delirious night,
He mutters Prince Lodalga's name, and sighs.
And sometimes, when the day's disdainful light
Floods the cold marble walls, he turns wan eyes
Upon his slaves, and asks that, ere he dies,
They grant one boon — one boon, and only one:
To let him see once more his best loved son."

With a low moan, Lodalga turned away.
Stricken and gasping, like a wounded hare,
Rash as a madman, with no word to say,
But teeth that gnashed in frenzy and despair
He reeled into the blown December air,
Where big flakes pelted . . . Through the gloom outside
Laughter rang out while jeering storm-winds cried.

III

Week after week he trod a tireless course
Over the plain into the rising sun,
With countenance seamed by sorrow and remorse,
Whereon a new regret had fought and won
A wasting war. And he conferred with none,
Except to ask what news the couriers brought,
And if the gods had smiled on Helmud's court.

But always woeful tidings spurred him on.
The king was drooping — so dispatches read.
And some predicted that the coming dawn
Would see black wreaths about the royal bed.
Then, brooding on the leagues and leagues ahead,
The prince would sigh, and long to rush through space
Wing-footed, at the bounding grayhound's pace.

Through hill-lands barred with deepening drifts of snow,
And lone sheep-ranges where the wind went mad,
And bridgeless torrents foaming to overflow,
And shadow-peopled valleys, cedar-clad,
He hastened on and on, too hurt and sad
To dread the wolf-packs howling in the night
Or care if storm-clouds roared or day shone bright.

Back on the trail of perished hopes he pressed,
Back from the far adventure he had craved.
But why return from the green-canyoned west
To the drab court where he had lain enslaved?
Still he despised the honors he had waived,
The silken robe, the coronet — why then
Go dashing headlong into chains again?

There was a reason he had not designed,
A cause that burned within him from of old.
Deep in unthreaded mazes of his mind
The fingers of the past had stamped their mold,
Bidding some overbearing mistress hold
His spirit in a childhood-woven spell
That piled-up years might dim but not dispel.

And still his reverence for his king and sire
Lay like a haunting shadow on his heart.
And old remembrance was a quenchless fire
Whose arrowy, stinging flames would hiss and dart,
Shedding pale rays on many an ancient part
That Helmud played. And in Lodalga's eyes
Dead moments like beseeching ghosts would rise.

And still he saw the sovereign when he bent
Moist-eyed above his queenly consort's bier;
And still he heard his father's sobbed lament
At a loved daughter's lightning-nipped career;
And out of happier hours he could hear
Shouting and laughter, when the monarch played
With merry sons by the palace colonnade.

And all the faded scenes rebuked him still,
Their tendrils clinging, tightening round his breast,
Most desolating when, against his will,
Pictures were framed before him, and oppressed
With visions of an old man's sore unrest,
His trenched and yellowing features like a plea
To one he sought and nevermore would see.

Even now, the long-drawn dirges might be sung;
Peach-blossoms might be shrivelling on his tomb.
And was there time to beat the clap of doom
And ease the storm and fever which had wrung
That agéd heart, and hear that well-known tongue
Whisper in gladness? Was there time to bare
His own remorse, and calm the king's despair?

Beneath the fires of his restored devotion,
Lit by live embers of the smoldering past,
Old feuds were quenched in a tender-fierce emotion,
And rancor died upon a cleansing blast.
And he forgot the clouds that overcast
His father's love, but looked on him anew
Like a young child for whom all skies are blue.

And as, with anxious steps, for endless hours,
He trudged and sweated on the barren road,
He dreamt no longer of the snow-white towers
Of steepled mountains or the debt he owed
To show the pool where mirrored Knowledge glowed.
Someday he would resume the thankless quest,
But now black dread would suffer him no rest.

IV

When fields were green, and orange flowers were blooming,
The lonely wanderer, worn of limb and mind,
Beheld afar those agate columns looming
That once in furious flight he left behind.
And still the crystal domes were golden-lined!
And, through the years that sundered and estranged,
Those carven spires and arches shone unchanged!

Unchanged! when all besides was marred and altered!
When his whole life was withering to decay!
Sadly, with flowing eyes, and steps that faltered,
He plodded on his grave, unnoted way,
Dream-held, while from far Persia and Cathay
Long caravans wound by, and camel teams
Jolted to town in never-ending streams.

At last he too, amid the boisterous throng,
Drifted, unchallenged, past the city wall.
And, once within, he would not dally long
To seek a well-remembered sea-green hall.
But at the gate he heard a sentry call,
"Back, rogue!", and paused to find a brandished blade
Flashing an order meant to be obeyed.

"Back, rogue!" again the irate guardian roared,
Scanning the ragged prince in wry disdain.
And menace crackled in his eyes; his sword
Gleamed sharply, while Lodalga pled in vain:
"Good friend, I crossed the enormous western plain
To see King Helmud — " Here he was cut short
By laughter mocking like an edged retort.

"Oh! So the king has nothing else to do
Than chat with beggars!" Now the swinging steel
Drew close, as though to slash the intruder through,
And all his words were like a child's appeal.
And, pleading still, Lodalga turned on heel,
While helmeted guards, each with a pointed pike,
Watched his gaunt form as though about to strike.

From gate to gate he flitted, like a shade
Escaped from Hades to the living land.
And, not less friendless than a ghost, he strayed
Where none would smile or lift a brotherly hand,
And none would pause to hear, or understand
That this rude vagrant, garbed in faded brown,
Could have a private message for the crown.

"Madman!" they dubbed him, as a myriad tongues
Had chorused during all the long, sad years.
And he might soon have screamed with bursting lungs
And gained a dungeon, where no freeman's ears
Could heed his groans, no touch assuage his tears;
And four stone walls might have become his grave,
But for a friend — an old forgotten slave.

Skirting the royal courtyard, where the hounds
Tugged at brass chains with lips that snarled and curled,
He saw a gray, bent man who made his rounds
Among the kennels, whistling low, and hurled
Bones to the pack . . . And now, from some lost world,
Stray recognition, with a bolt of light,
Flashed pictures out of memory's cavern-night.

Where had he seen that shambling form before —
That tawny, pockmarked face and thinning hair?
Suddenly, through the years that were no more,
He saw himself upon the palace stair,
A red-cheeked lad, while with a weighty air
The king's chief gardener, at his pleas, related
Old dragon tales he breathlessly awaited.

"Norval!" he muttered, as the servant's name
Burst back on him across the void of years . . .
He heard a gasp; and all the gardener's frame
Shuddered, and his pale eyes were brimmed with tears.
"But can this be? Can I believe my ears?"
He shouted, while his shocked, inquiring eyes
Fell on the wanderer's rags in stunned surprise.

"Lodalga! O young Master, is it you?
The voice is yours! The face is scarce your own!"
And as the quivering prince replied, "It's true!"
Impulsively affectionate arms were thrown
About his shoulders; and two warm eyes shown
In happy greeting. "Welcome back, my Lord!
We need you, need your scepter and your sword!

"We need you, for the empire has no head
And soulless claimants wrangle for the crown!"
"And is my father living, then — or dead?"
Lodalga gasped . . . But with bleak eyes bent down
And brow contracted in a desolate frown
Norval announced, "The king still lives, they say,
But sinks and sinks, while thousands weep and pray.

"And if you'd do him homage ere he lies
Speechless and stiff, cold on the casket stone,
You must make haste, for he may close his eyes
Even before another sun has shone."
"Then help me!" begged Lodalga, with a moan.
"Find me some royal vestments, to convince
The world I'm not a scullion, but a prince!"

"I'll try," said Norval, with a scowl. "I'll try,
May the gods help us! Wait for me a space."
And off he flitted — and the sun moved high
While forward and backward, at a nervous pace,
Lodalga strode. Upon his shrunken face
Lay that sharp torment, worse than barbs of steel,
Which only the self-afflicting soul may feel.

Hours had gone . . . Late in the waning day,
Norval returned. In whispers he began,
"Follow, my Lord! Perhaps I've found a way!
I've won the king's high stewart to a plan
To baffle the palace guardsmen — if we can.
Some clothing, and a blade to shear your head,
Lie hidden there — in yonder cattle shed."

It was a new Lodalga that emerged
All crimson-gowned, again a monarch's son,
As though the frills and periwig had purged
His life of all unkingly deeds he'd done.
Cringe low, you sentries! Let him bow to none!
His cloak was silk, a sword hung at his side,
And velvet headdress capped his sovereign pride.

Boldly, and with a brisk and haughty mien,
He hastened where drawn lances had beset
An hour before. And now a duke or queen
Might not have matched the reverence that he met.
The sabres which had waved an arrogant threat
Drooped in obeisance; a fawning corps
Of sentinels swung wide the palace door.

V

There was a darkness in the royal room
That mumbling priestly lips could not abate.
Dim tapers flickered; in an ashen gloom
Courtiers and guards, like statues, stood in wait,
While a black shadow, like close-hovering fate,
Stalked over all, with greedy arms outspread
For one who moaned and panted on the bed.

Restless he lay, with fearsome, glaring eyes
In cup-like sockets, blue and crater-deep,
Gaping as though at undiscovered skies
Beyond the fast-approaching shore of sleep.
And ghastly fingerprints appeared to creep
Along the pinched white cheek and brow, and trace
An ominous presence on the bony face.

Silence like chill foreboding overhung
The violet canopies and marble hall,
Save when, with sagging lips and parching tongue,
The sick man groaned, or, faltering, tried to call
That he was cold, and some tense lord or thrall
Darted to do his bidding . . . Time went by
Slowly as though the stricken world must die.

For hours the king had muttered scarce a word,
But panting no longer, lay inert as wood.
Then, at the door, a rush and stir was heard,
And looming in the light a stranger stood.
"A prince would like to see you, if he could,"
Announced a gateman. "Sire, it's all too clear
Some high momentous mission brings him here."

"I speak with none," the monarch muttered low.
"Let him who loves a dungeon disobey!"
With a long sigh, he turned his gaze away,
Yet did not hear the late arrival go.
But weirdly, in the wavering candle glow,
He saw a tall form tower, like a shade
His old vain prayers and mocking hopes had made.

And two bright eyes were fixed upon his own,
And two great arms were raised in mute distress,
And on the luminous face a strange light shone,
And lips, fast-clenched, were struggling to repress
Gasps of despair; a trembling eagerness
Shook the thin shape. Amid the gathering haze
King Helmud watched with fascinated gaze.

And long he stared and stared, until it seemed
That gibbering phantoms of the years gone by
Gathered to jeer and flout him while he dreamed.
But what was that — that sudden tortured cry?
"Father!" — And did his senses merely lie?
"Father!" — And at that word his icy hands
Swayed in a grip as though of iron bands.

"Father!" — and need he longer doubt or fear?
The light came back into his clouded mind;
Anthems of angels sounded in his ear,
And he forgot the wounding days behind.
"My son, Lodalga! Surely I was blind
Not to observe you!" And his withered face
Grew damp, his frail arms met a fierce embrace.

Then a low thankful sobbing racked his frame,
And on his cheeks a feverish crimson burned.
"My son, what epochs passed before you came,
Though many a time I dreamt you had returned
And won anew the father's love you spurned!
Where were you hiding? Why, these cruel years,
Leave us to fading hope and sterile fears?"

The sufferer coughed and coughed, with heaving chest
And lungs that gasped and painfully fought for air.
But passion blazed, and would not be repressed,
And unobservant of his son's despair
And shuddering councillors entreating care,
He struggled to resume, "What matter now
Where you have wandered? Make today one vow,

"And I'll forgive the heartache and the wrong
Of all the iron and remorseless days.
Only one vow — the time cannot be long.
Grant me that when I walk the shadowed ways
I may remember you with joy and praise."
"What vow, my father?" asked the moist-cheeked son.
"Speak, and I swear your bidding shall be done!"

"The empire wanes," King Helmud slowly said.
"Your brothers, pleasure-softened, fawn and fight
To win the crown — yet for the kingdom's head
There's only one firm-sceptered hand in sight.
The throne is yours by duty and by right,
My eldest son — so take it while you can
And let me die a well-contented man."

Lodalga heard in silence; and the king,
Waxing more eager, sat erect in bed,
Frail arms uplifted. "Promise but this thing:
You'll hunt no more chimeras, but, instead,
Remain in court, and rule when I am dead.
Grant me this boon!" His forced, disconsolate plea
Glared from his bloodshot eyes distractedly.

But still, with lips compressed and knotted brow,
Lodalga stared and could not make reply.
The king's hand trembled. "Come, one vow — one vow!"
He begged, and with a deep, half-moaning sigh
Sank back upon his couch. And every eye
Flashed horror, when he shivered, gave a start
And clutched with desperate fingers at his heart.

"I promise, father — hear, I promise all!"
Lodalga cried. And, with a smothered groan,
"I promise!" But could frenzied words recall
The soul fast-leaving for some ampler zone?
The stricken man grew still; and lying prone
On the dishevelled sheets, he faintly spoke,
"Bless you, my son . . . respect the kingly cloak . . .

"Bless you . . . my son — " The murmur trailed away
Into the dark; and shuddery tremors smote
The wasted frame; and from the unbared throat
Dread rattlings rose — then stiff and still he lay.
The watchers gasped; a few began to pray,
While, with convulsive moans, one mourner knelt,
Grasping a crumpled form, which neither saw nor felt.

Part IV

DISENCHANTMENT

I

The reign of King Lodalga was renowned
For golden flowering of a thousand arts,
Though rarely, in his realm, one heard the sound
Of sabres clashing, and not many hearts
Were torn by driven swords or hurtled darts.
And since he swung no lance except for law,
He was a king not widely held in awe.

Had he been governed by the council room
And not recoiled at brothers torn and slain
When, marching fifty thousand men to doom
With bugles blaring triumph, one can gain
Less than the nod of friendship might obtain —
Ah, then how nobly he'd have led the state,
While doting myriads knelt, and called him great.

And had he headed some fire-hurling band
To save the kingdom from its smaller foes,
Whipped screaming peoples from a smoking land,
Felled babes and mothers with bowel-ripping bows,
And left but ash-heaps where he found the rose,
Then fond disciples might have reared a shrine
Sacred to "Great Lodalga, Lord Divine."

But all his roads were avenues of peace;
He bade his spidery diplomats retire,
Ordered that tournaments and war-games cease,
And honored the player of the harp and lyre.
No roving minstrel need, unheard, require
Pence from the royal purse; no bard need fear
His sovereign's deafness or a sentry's spear.

But scribes made many books, and painters flourished,
And art was hailed above the huckster's lore,
Weavers of Odyssean dreams were cherished,
And beauty chanted songs at every door,
Till earth was nearer heaven than before.
And yet Lodalga's rule, for all these gains,
Lacked the repute of storm-and-thunder reigns.

The king, men said, had weakling moods that gave
Unroyal looks to many a royal deed.
He would not pose, nor let red pennants wave
When he went cantering on his white-plumed steed.
He would not govern by a granite creed,
Nor let the people, cowering at his nod,
Pile him an altar, kneel to him as god.

But he was friend to all: the slave and priest,
Merchant and beggar were as one to him.
And once he honored, at a palace feast,
Two vagabonds that made his eyes grow dim
By picturing peaks beyond the Western rim;
And once men saw him ambling through the town
Jesting with peasants . . . in a peasant's gown.

Wise were the laws he gave, and few denied
The poor were less like nags beneath the yoke,
The strong less heavy-corseleted in their pride
Than when his fathers wore the royal cloak.
And he was true as steel — yet how invoke
His name with that god-reverence one would grant
The heart or head of brass or adamant?

What was he really like, this humble king
For whom a scepter was a leaden weight,
For whom the daisies and the grass of spring
Had deeper glory than the deeds of state?
Often, in throne-rooms of the gilded great
And straw-roofed huts of herdsmen, rumor stalked
With viper stings, and rattling gossips talked.

So it was bruited that Lodalga's life
Was overcast by many a sullen cloud.
Some said he had a vixen queen for wife,
Shallow as dregs and hence superbly proud.
And some, with furtive covered lips, avowed
He wed — with protests — but to gain an heir,
And loved his spouse as rabbits love a snare.

And others, telling how the king at night
Haunted, alone, the palace parapet,
Swore that he rambled as a sentinel might
Forward and back, with sighs as of regret.
And some discovered that his eyes were wet
When he recalled a mystic pool that lay
High in the sunset mountains, worlds away.

II

What could men know of lurking fires that burned
Under the breast that bore the kingly star? —
Of that impassioned heart, which turned and turned,
Hopelessly fettered, to the crags afar?
No falcon pinioned by a wired bar
Ever beat fiercer wings for freedom flown
Than did this monarch shackled to a throne.

Caught like a felon struggling to escape!
Year after year his futile breath might last,
Yet he must spread a funeral wreath and crepe
Over the murdered glories of the past.
Youth, and youth's aspirations, must be cast
Into a burial vault, and he must be
Pinioned by pomp and steel-necked dignity.

For how can one who wields a royal rod
And hears an empire's jangling fears and cares,
Do homage to a mountain-shadowed god
Or set a foot on starry thoroughfares?
The din of querulous needs and small despairs
Must fill his ears; the iron of the mart
Must form strait-jackets tightening round his heart.

And after mounting into snow-tipped skies
And scaling crags where eagles sank to rest,
He must become as hosts whom life denies
The wide horizons of a nobler quest —
Save when remembrance murmured in his breast
And half revived, above the bawling throng,
The torturing sweetness of an old, lost song.

Deeply Lodalga rued his royal rank.
As one who, slipping on a mountainside,
Grabs at a glassy rock's projecting flank
But misses, sees a cavern opening wide,
And, helpless, feels himself begin to slide —
So did the king, on some abysmal slope,
Stumble, and lift fierce arms in fruitless hope.

Still, as the years went by, his dreams would dwell
Less often on the peaks' stone-ribbed array.
If from the deeps his old regrets would well,
They flowed less freely, in a devious way.
And all his thoughts grew desolate and gray,
And in a moody reminiscent vein
He looked for salve to soothe his lingering pain.

"I sought to kindle lamps that could not shine,
I sought to rear a citadel in air.
No other eyes can gaze upon the shrine,
No other feet ascend the glacial stair.
I pleaded to a world that did not care,
And if I preached a hundred thousand years
Men still would blindly pass, with muffled ears.

"Yet what if others dare not mount the peak
Or catch the luminous vision I have caught?
They may be happier not to strive or seek,
But, like wise oxen, leave the fight unfought,
Nor fish in seas of doubt for pearls of thought . . .
Earthworms that twist and tunnel through the night
May be more fortunate not to see the light."

So would Lodalga muse when wakening dawn
Lit a red taper in the misty sky,
Or when illumined drapes of day were drawn
Back from the stars, which rode augustly by
Like prophets of the truth that cannot die.
And in this ashen mood, he grew resigned
To leave the watchtowers of the past behind —

Resigned to lolling in a marble seat,
Seeing the years trail past in slow parade,
Counting the nation's crop of flax or wheat
Or yields of caravans or sea-borne trade,
Or planning how, with arms and plaques displayed,
To greet a royal guest, or how a feud
Might be restrained or border tribes subdued.

A thousand tasks he mastered with the skill
And mulish plodding given to kings and slaves
When the wild heart is bridled by the will
And the torn mind forsakes the bourn it craves.
The vision of the sunset-glimmering waves
And snowy Kunglas now but seldom came
To stir his pulse and prod a weakening aim.

And as the cold, Lethean fogs of time
Closed on horizons he could not regain,
He half forgot the spurs that bade him climb
To the bright pinnacles, and groped in vain
For some forgotten pilot in his brain,
Trying to find the path his feet had pressed
To the weird Knowledge on the mountain's crest.

The secret passed him like a comet's flight!
He could not picture what his eyes had seen!
Only that he had glimpsed immortal light
Which, ghostlike, faded in the years between!
What were the truths that he had thought to glean
From the still waters? Had they been no more
Than wind-marks printed on a sandy shore?

Gone! And he was as one who never gazed,
In the lone star-time, at a twinkling lake.
The world-enveloping raptures that had blazed,
The glimpses into beauty that would make
Music to soothe the hammering doubt and ache
Of every sufferer's heart — these had been lost
Like foam-flecks where the ocean beat and tossed.

Forty long years — burdened yet empty years —
Imposed their leaden shadows on the past.
And in the clash of councils and careers,
The plots and bickerings that overcast
His courtly life, Lodalga came at last
Not only to believe old splendor fled
But scarcely to lament the vision dead.

Forty disheartening years! Their crookéd hands
Had shaped the monarch with a clawing hold.
His glistening eyes shone softer than of old
Above a beard traversed by granite bands;
His pain-scarred countenance, where a thousand brands
Had scorched an imprint, glowered like the mask
Of one resigned to some heartrending task.

Forty blind years! The inescapable lot
Of kings and clowns lay like a cat in wait.
Now he was weary, weary — could he not
Lighten his load before the ultimate Date?
Too long his hands had clutched the bronze of state,
Too long! and he was tired — and he sighed
For freedom that his jeweled chains defied.

A few more fights, a few more gilded schemes,
A few more sips of honey, wine, or gall,
A few more hungerings and desert dreams,
And then the certain end — and was that all? —
His fate the nothingness that must befall
The earthworm and the spider? What the gain
From the salt years of his bewildering reign?

Barren, more barren than a storm-combed beach,
This life once irised with luxuriant flowers,
This life that, long before, had seemed to reach
Beyond the shadow of man's fleeting hours
To grandeur of sky-piercing cones and towers
And blue eternity! Had he but slaved
To blaze his hallmark where the billows raved?

How many a man, still crownless and unsought,
Might kindle brighter lanterns round the throne,
While he, amid the fumings of the court,
Had lost the spark inquiring youth had known!
And yet — and yet — could he not half atone?
Casting away his sceptered mien and might,
Could he not gain again the faded light?

What if he struggled up the peak once more,
Feasted his spirit on the mirrored blue,
Relearned the secrets he had quaffed before
And in exuberant worship, drank anew
From bottomless wells whereon the ages drew?
Only a mist, a dream? And yet the ache
Of the void years made buried hope awake.

Importunate ghosts of his dead youth arose
And beckoned to the far, abandoned trail.
And he had glimpses of the moonlit snows
And sun upon the silver-clouded vale,
And heard the pandemonium of the gale.
And day by day the teasing thought came back
Of the untraveled upward-looping track.

III

But he might fruitlessly have mulled and planned
With the slow pulse of age that will not dare,
And his dim eyes would nevermore have scanned
The jagged white-domes arching high in air,
But with gaunt fingers clutching in despair
At marble walls, he would have yearned and died
Had a weird dream not come to stir and guide.

It seemed he sat upon a rosebud throne,
Where mummers danced and tasselled slaves bowed down,
When, high above, two eyeless sockets shone
Out of a shadowy skull; two hands of bone
Reached nakedly forward, fumbling for his crown.
And a faint crackling laughter, echo-thin,
Startled his ears above the revelers' din.

Then, as the phosphorescent arms drew near
And he, in horror, could not move or speak,
And hollow eye-holes fixed him with a leer,
And frigid fingers brushed his throat and cheek,
Suddenly from the fleshless lips a shriek
Shrilled in loud menace. And thereon a screen
Was lifted from the whole macabre scene.

The skeleton arms were gone, the grisly face
Had vanished, and the throne-room slid from sight,
But moonlit waters glimmered in their place
And gray crags shouldered high into the night.
And on the topmost ledge there gleamed a light
Like a wind-shaken torch; it flashed and waved
As though to mark the bourn Lodalga craved.

Like a great torch, above the peaks it glowed,
And mild blue woman's eyes began to shine,
While over the ice Lodalga traced a road
Spiralling heavenward, a luminous line.
And womanly arms were lifted, as a sign
To mount and follow; and there came a voice:
"The palace or the peak — yours still to make the choice."

Part VII

THE FINAL QUEST

I

The choice was made. Lodalga trudged once more
The sweaty, clattering highway of the plain,
As he had trudged it fifty years before
When, as a youth, he hungered to attain
The far horizon, and the clouds' domain.
But though his face had still a wistful glow,
His back was stooping, and his gait was slow.

Garbed in a nomad's dusty flannel gown,
With knapsack dangling, and an oaken rod,
He hardly looked like one to claim a crown;
But through the hollows of the cracking sod
And over sandy barrens he would plod,
Eyes downward, and with open arms that pled
Often in vain to win a beggar's bread.

Not seldom, when the bleeding sun would set
Beyond brown pastures, in a crimson void,
He would remember — scarcely with regret —
How his imperial staff had been destroyed.
He would recall the ruses he employed
When, with a peddler's turban for disguise,
He had escaped beneath the sentries' eyes —

Escaped, as in remote and sturdier days,
Picking the path his youthful feet had known.
Now, where enameled lamps shed brazen rays,
His eldest son would pose upon the throne . . .
The lock was turned, the fatal seed was sown,
And as he passed the armorial gate, he knew
The key was gone, forever gone from view.

A crownless monarch, veiled and mourned as dead!
Daily the leagues grew further from the court;
Daily, on blistered feet, he pushed ahead
Nearer the snowy spires his youth had sought.
And months went by — it seemed he had refought
Half the sad battles of forgotten years
In thorns and mire, and with his doubt and fears,

In thorns and mire, and on the houseless road,
With wild beasts, brigands, and his own remorse . . .
And other months went by . . . Lodalga strode
To the dim west on an uncertain course.
At times his purpose fluttered, lost its force;
At times he strained and panted, but his gaze
Still bent in longing on the sunset blaze.

For still he dreamed the ultimate peak would make
His days resplendent with a mellowing light;
And with fond pictures of the mountain lake
He warmed his chilly heart, and found the might
To flounder onward, till at last the sight
Of far blue ranges bade the fires of hope
Burn fiercely, and he swore to dare the slope.

So once again he took a sinuous path,
Looping beneath the stolid peak and crag,
Where storm-winds sneered and pelted, shrill with wrath,
And, on some soggy grade, his feet would drag
And he would falter like a smitten stag,
Longing to lie, stone-silent, on the floor
Of the soft snow, and yearn and dream no more.

But still some fading ember of his strength
Shone in his heart, and with the power that flows
From the unconquered self, he came at length
To where, amid the never-melting snows,
A well remembered, lonely peak arose,
Eternal Kungla, on whose icy spire
Shimmered the waters of his life's desire.

All was unaltered! When in youth he came,
Robust of stride, to keep a self-made vow,
Those battered rocky bastions were the same,
The same woods glowered from the mountain's brow.
All was unaltered, save that winter now
Mantled the world, and not alone the height
But many a deep-cut valley gleamed in white.

Long and forlornly King Lodalga stared
At that bold summit where the timeless shone.
And hours had drifted by before he dared
To set his footprints on the steps of stone.
Then, racked by an occasional gasp or groan,
Unconfident of returning, he essayed
The long ascent, but still delayed, delayed.

Yet new excited flurries stirred his heart,
And in his veins the blood more quickly flowed,
And he was moved by part, though only part
Of those hot raptures which in youth had glowed
And held him to the bare and friendless road.
And from within a voice still seemed to call,
"The peak! The peak! You must not fail or fall!"

Step by worn step, as in the days long dead,
He struggled up the spiny lava lane,
With limbs that sagged, and battered feet that bled,
And tortured mind grown desperate to retain
A sanguine mood, while aching eyes would strain
To that rock-tower which guarded at its breast
The immortal waters of his passionate quest.

Slow was his gait; his breath came short and fast;
Often he rested on the forest floor.
And would some snow-drift be his home — the last,
While mockingly, high above, the peak would soar?
Sometimes, when cannonading gales would roar
Or writhing floods defied him, it would seem
The pool was but a dream within a dream.

And sometimes, when he fought his slippery way
On ice-beaked ledges, grappling for a hold,
Or over misty cliffs that seemed to say,
"Never a passage here for one so old!"
Then he would know that he was over-bold
To dare the hazardous summit, and would long
For safer highways, trodden by the throng.

But his was now a trail of no returning —
The path before him, and the open sky,
He could but bow before the master yearning
To gain the pool, or, seeking it, to die.
Up, up he trudged, with many a pause and sigh,
And up and up, now slower, slower still,
With reeling limbs, and stern but staggering will.

By night he sought some cavern's black recess
Where the lean panther may have nursed her brood.
Or in a piny canyoned wilderness,
Or hunched amid a frozen solitude
Where night winds beat him in a weeping mood,
He lit his campfire, then would numbly creep
Under his bearskin robe for broken sleep.

Five days went by, and lengthened into ten,
Ten days of warfare with the rocks and snow,
Ten days of heartache, till he reached again
The last ascent beneath that high plateau
Where smiled the waters he had pined to know.
Ah, for the thrust, the impetus of his prime!
Now his worn limbs had scarcely strength to climb.

Blocked! and he might have fallen; gained for bed
The ice and silence of a deep crevasse.
But as he labored, strangely overhead
He saw, beneath the jutting granite mass,
A dim-marked stair whose windings seemed to pass
Over the cliff, as though benignly planned
For weary climbers by some human hand.

Another hour of grappling with the slope,
And then the pool's blue eye and icicled shore!
Yet, rising like the murderer of hope,
A freezing gale began to screech once more;
And down upon him, cloud on cloud, it bore
The demon-tempered legions of the snow,
As if to warn, "Make haste, make haste below!"

Then must he perish, or turn round and fail?
Must he, within an arm's reach of his mark,
Falter, and let the talons of the gale
Buffet him like a sparrow down the dark?
He would not, could not pause! Some dormant spark
Of fire long burnt to ash came flaring back
And drew him to the hard, wind-challenged track.

Skirting high drifts, he plodded on a course
Above the sheer white void — a crawling form,
A tottering mote that barely had the force
To breast the persecution of the storm.
Only the hearth within him kept him warm,
Defying the jagged steeps; an inner light
Gave to his failing limbs some outer might.

And with a power replenished from his will
And that desire which cannot brook defeat,
He panted up the craggy stairway still,
His heart protesting, skipping many a beat,
His spirit feverish with a blazing heat
That spurred him forth and on . . . And now at last
The snowstorm ceased, the clouds themselves were passed.

And night came on — but with the night it seemed
Another stride would lift him to his goal.
Wanly upon the snow the starlight beamed,
With ghost-reflections from a glacial bowl
Between rock-peaks . . . when suddenly the whole
Of his steep climb was done. As long ago,
He stood upon a narrow-necked plateau —

That weird plateau beneath the tapering cone,
Cradling the lake of blue immortal light.
But where — where was the glory he had known?
Where was the pool? Had he turned dull of sight?
Were there no waters sparkling crystal-bright
Under lit heavens? Surely, he was blind!
Black veiling vapors had befogged his mind!

With senses blurred, he could but gape and strain,
Bewildered, and his blinking eyes could see
Mere shadowy cliff-walls and a shut-off plain
Above the snowbanks mounded drearily,
While frost was glittering in malicious glee
With points of impish laughter, and the gale
Derisively began to lunge and wail.

Near stupefied, he prayed, and praying, thought
The quick staccato of his pulse would stop.
Those dim-remembered waters he had sought
Perhaps were on some other mountaintop.
Then, in despair, he almost wished to drop
Over the ridge to kind forgetfulness,
And lose his wearying doubt and old distress,

And be enveloped in the mighty peace
That wrapped the ranges in a robe of awe,
Silent, where trials and hurt desires would cease
Under the sovereignty of ageless law.
And brooding thus, he stirred a pace, and saw
New apparitions in the shocked surprise
With which a shade may greet incredulous eyes.

A polished ice-sheet, with an oval floor,
Spread in long even curves amid the snow.
And white, unearthly white the rug it wore,
Such as a marbled palace court may show,
A flawless white projecting far below
Beneath white terraces that seemed to grace
The vestibule of some celestial place.

The pool at last! The longed-for pool at last!
Frozen and blank, its summer wizardry flown!
Winter had draped the world; the sleety blast
Had turned it lifeless as a pond of stone.
Yet from its breast unearthly lanterns shone;
And as he stared, the wanderer gave a sigh —
An icy moon peeped from an icy sky.

And then — what fever in his brain was this?
What apparition of his failing sight?
What surging warmth of unexpected bliss
While great forms gathered in the spectral light,
Of whom the tallest, of a hillock's height,
Pointed a long arm skyward to a shape
Clad in a pearly white archangel's cape.

And, thunder-toned but musical, a voice
Called in his ears: "For him who pants and seeks
The quest goes on! The Warders give a choice:
The valley flat-land, or the snows and peaks.
Only in his own heart the answer speaks,
And he who rightly chooses finds a gate
Beyond the dusk, where mightier waters wait."

The searcher's hand reached out; entranced he stood
At some ethereal vision, and he smiled
As if a spokesman of immortal good
Uttered a summons from the craggy wild,
Where rock on rock and drift on drift was piled.
And sinking suddenly at some mute command,
He knew a touch like some fond mother's hand.

Again he saw a light, a torch that glowed,
And mild blue woman's eyes began to shine.
Far over the ice Lodalga traced a road
Spiralling heavenward, a luminous line.
And while a prone form marked a snow-incline,
The freed adventurer felt himself arise
To look for brighter pools beneath more radiant skies.

THE END